JAN. 1, 2008
STRATEGIST

*To create his army of volunteers,
Obama worked to energize groups like
this one, at a gym in Davenport, Iowa*

TIME

MANAGING EDITOR Richard Stengel
ART DIRECTOR Arthur Hochstein
CHIEF PICTURE EDITOR Alice Gabriner

President Obama:
The Path to the White House

EDITOR Adi Ignatius
DESIGNER Sharon Okamoto
ASSOCIATE PICTURE EDITORS Crary Pullen, Leslie dela Vega
CHIEF REPORTER Deirdre van Dyk
EDITORIAL PRODUCTION Lionel P. Vargas
COPY EDITOR Joseph McCombs

TIME INC. HOME ENTERTAINMENT

PUBLISHER Richard Fraiman
GENERAL MANAGER Steven Sandonato
EXECUTIVE DIRECTOR, MARKETING SERVICES Carol Pittard
DIRECTOR, RETAIL & SPECIAL SALES Tom Mifsud
DIRECTOR, NEW PRODUCT DEVELOPMENT Peter Harper
ASSISTANT DIRECTOR, NEWSSTAND MARKETING Laura Adam
ASSISTANT DIRECTOR, BRAND MARKETING Joy Butts
ASSOCIATE COUNSEL Helen Wan
SENIOR BRAND MANAGER, TWRS/M Holly Oakes
BOOK PRODUCTION MANAGER Suzanne Janso
DESIGN & PREPRESS MANAGER Anne-Michelle Gallero
ASSOCIATE BRAND MANAGER Michela Wilde

SPECIAL THANKS TO:
Glenn Buonocore, Susan Chodakiewicz, Margaret Hess, Brynn Joyce, Robert Marasco, Richard Prue, Brooke Reger, Mary Sarro-Waite, Ilene Schreider, Adriana Tierno, Alex Voznesenskiy

Copyright © 2008 Time Inc. Home Entertainment
Published by TIME Books, Time Inc. • 1271 Avenue of the Americas • New York, NY 10020

ISBN 10: 1-60320-072-X
ISBN 13: 978-1-60320-072-1
Library of Congress Number: 2008909716

We welcome your comments and suggestions about TIME Books. Please write to us at:
TIME Books, Attention: Book Editors, P.O. Box 11016, Des Moines, IA 50336-1016

If you would like to order any of our hardcover Collector's Edition books, please call us at 1-800-327-6388 (Monday through Friday, 7:00 a.m.– 8:00 p.m., or Saturday, 7:00 a.m.– 6:00 p.m., Central Time).

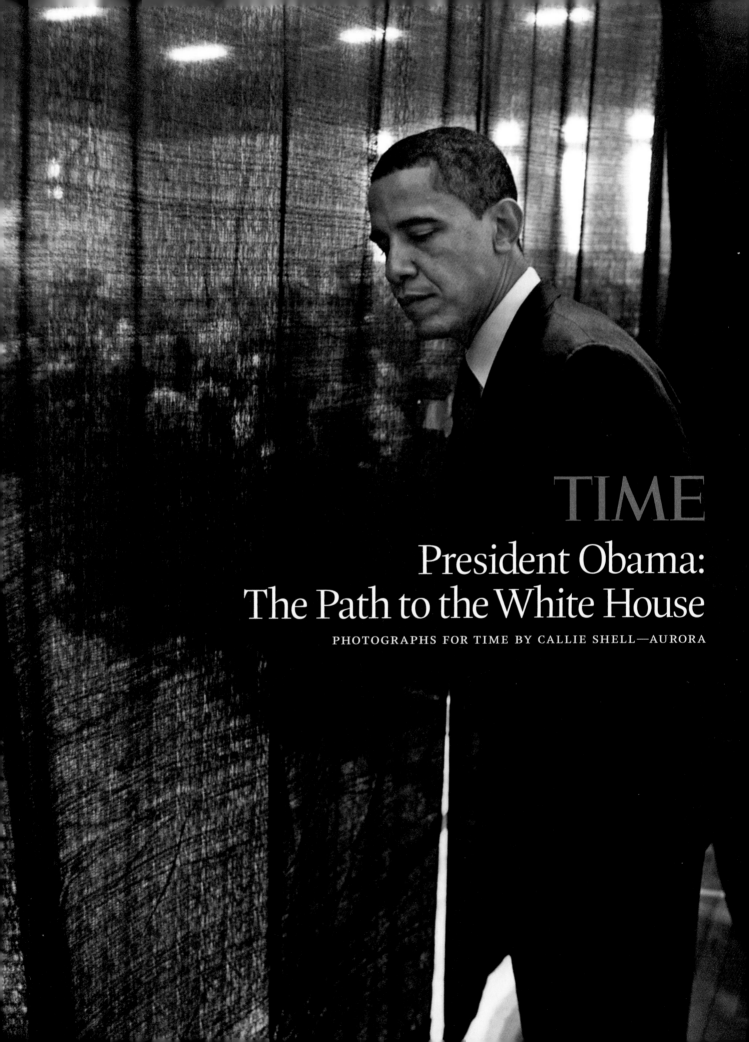

TIME

President Obama: The Path to the White House

PHOTOGRAPHS FOR TIME BY CALLIE SHELL—AURORA

Contents

PHOTOGRAPHS FOR TIME
BY CALLIE SHELL—AURORA

FEB. 16, 2007
THE ROCK STAR

Early in his run, Obama holds a rally at the
Columbia convention center in South Carolina
to explain why he wants to be President

Obama's Moment

The experts said he wasn't prepared, but Barack Obama found a way to connect with Americans ready for a new kind of candidate

BY RICHARD STENGEL

DEMOCRATIC PRESIDENTS TEND NOT TO WAIT their turn. People told John Kennedy and Jimmy Carter and Bill Clinton to wait four or even eight years to run. But those men knew something about themselves and something about the electorate, and in each of their campaigns, the man and the moment came together.

People also told Barack Obama to wait. It was Hillary Clinton's turn; he was too young; he had an unfamiliar name. But Obama knew something about himself and the nation he hoped to lead. He knew America would be ready for him, even if the party elders were not. He followed a famous hockey player's advice and skated to where the puck would be, not where it had been.

Like those previous Democratic Presidents, Obama represents a paradigm shift. From the moment he appeared on the national scene, there was something different about him—and I mean more than that he was the child of a white woman from Kansas and a black man from Kenya. Like Kennedy, Carter and Clinton before him, he created a new political rhetoric. His calm thoughtfulness and even-keeled explanatory style was an antidote to our polarized, overheated politics. Unlike the famous appraisal of F.D.R.—that the New York aristocrat had a second-class mind but a first-class temperament— Obama seemed to have a first-class mind *and* a first-class temperament.

Photographer Callie Shell, whose work we showcase in this publication, also has a first-class temperament—and a first-class eye. She hails from South Carolina, and this is her fifth presidential campaign. Shell (that's her, above, with Obama) started covering the candidate for TIME in January 2006, when his traveling party numbered three people in a van: the driver, Obama and her. Since then, she has become, as an Obama staffer puts it, "part of the family." More than anyone else, shell has been able to show the private side of Obama, what he is like in repose, when he is not onstage or behind the podium. Shell's artistry reveals Obama's true self by showing him, unguarded, in places where almost no one gets to see him.

GRAND ENTRANCE *The newly elected First Couple at Chicago's Grant Field*

Nov. 7, 2007
Staging Ground

*Obama addresses a town-hall meeting in Burlington,
Iowa, part of a barnstorming tour across the state.
Two months later, he finishes first in the state's caucus*

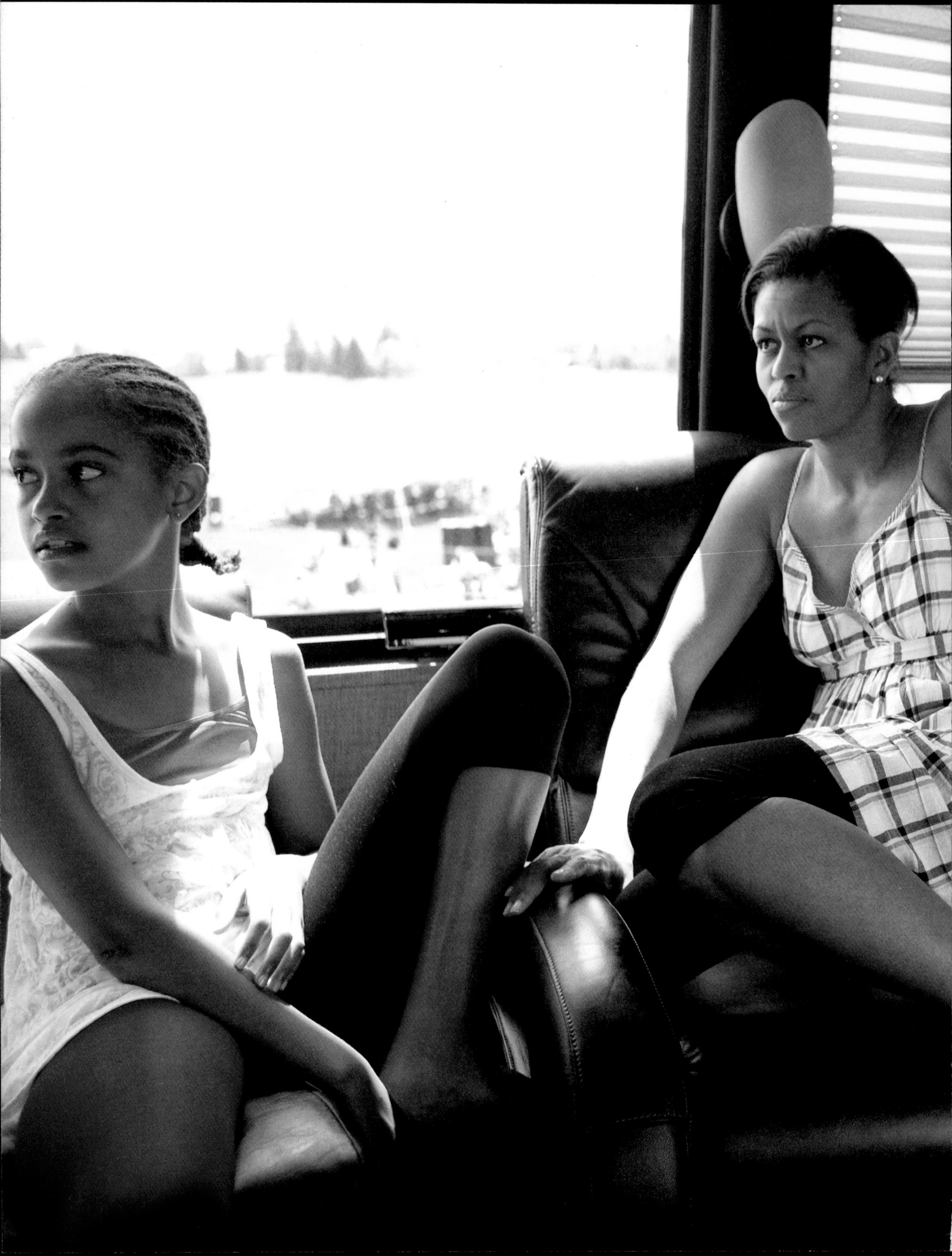

JULY 4, 2008
FAMILY TIME

*The Obamas curl up to watch a
hot-dog-eating contest on TV before attending
a picnic and parade in Butte, Mont.*

AUG. 29, 2008
BUILDING MOMENTUM

*A day after accepting the Democratic nomination, Obama,
with Michelle and running mate Joe Biden looking on, holds
a rally in Beaver in the battleground state of Pennsylvania*

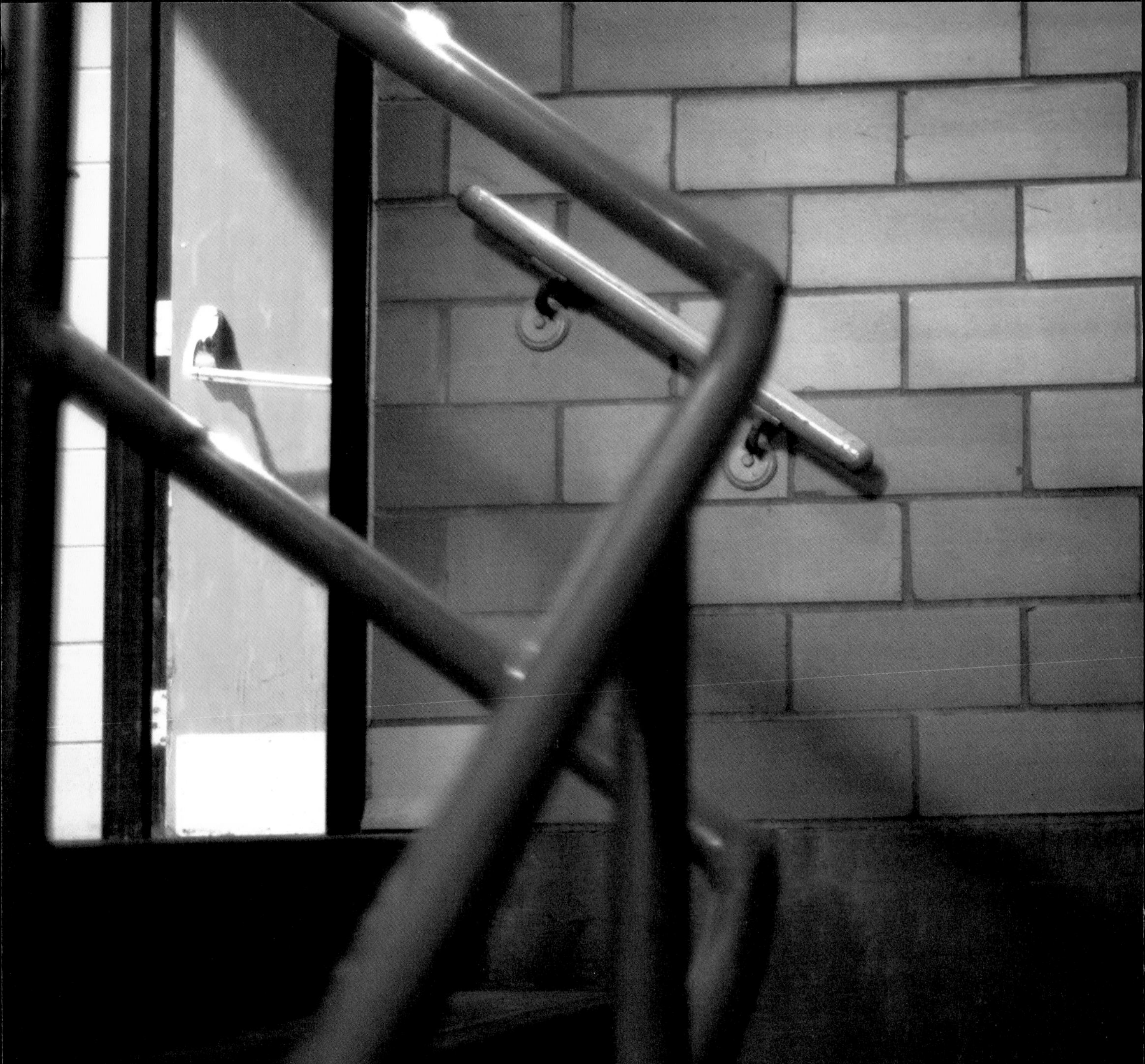

The Fresh Face

TIME first put Barack Obama on its cover in October 2006, saying the first-term Senator had the charisma and ambition to run for President. But he wasn't yet ready to answer the tough questions

By Joe Klein

O N A FRESH, SUNNY SATURDAY MORNING IN ROCKFORD, ILL., NEARLY A THOU-sand people have gathered in the gymnasium at Rock Valley College to participate in a town meeting with their Senator, Barack Obama. It is an astonishingly large crowd, but Obama has become an American political phenomenon in what seems about a nanosecond, and the folks are giddy with anticipation. "We know he's got the charisma," says Bertha McEwing, who has lived in Rockford for more than 50 years. "We want to know if he's got the brains." Just then there is a ripple through the crowd, then gasps, cheers and applause as Obama lopes into the gym with a casual, knees-y stride. "Missed ya," he says, moving to the microphone, and he continues greeting people over raucous applause. "*Tired* of Washington."

There's a sly hipster syncopation to his cadence, "Been *stuck* there for a while." But the folksiness disappears when he starts answering questions. Obama's actual speaking style is quietly conversational, low in rhetoric-saturated fat; there is no harrumph to him. About half-way through the hour-long meeting, a middle-aged man stands up and says what seems to be

MAKING A CONNECTION *Obama appealed to many white voters in part because he seemed to transcend racial stereotypes*

on everyone's mind, with appropriate passion: "Congress hasn't done a damn thing this year. I'm tired of the politicians blaming each other. We should throw them all out and start over!"

"Including me?" the Senator asks.

A chorus of *n-o-o-o-s.* "Not you," the man says. "You're brand new." Obama wanders into a casual disquisition about the sluggish nature of democracy. The answer is not even remotely a standard, pretaped political response. He moves through some fairly arcane turf, talking about how political gerrymandering has led to a generation of politicians who come from safe districts where they don't have to consider the other side of the debate, which has made compromise—and therefore legislative progress—more difficult. "That's why I favored Arnold Schwarzenegger's proposal last year, a nonpartisan commission to draw the congressional-district maps in California. Too bad it lost." The crowd is keeping up with Obama, listening closely as he segues into a detailed discussion of the federal budget. Eventually, he realizes he has been filibustering and apologizes to the crowd for "making a speech." No one seems to care, since Obama is doing something pretty rare in latter-day American politics: he is respecting their intelligence. He's a liberal, but not a screechy partisan. Indeed, he seems obsessively eager to find common ground with conservatives. "It's such a relief after all the screaming you see on TV," says Chuck Sweeny, political editor of the Rockford *Register Star.* "Obama is reaching out. He's saying the other side isn't evil. You can't imagine how powerful a message that is for an audience like this."

Obama's personal appeal is made manifest when he steps down from the podium and is swarmed by well-wishers of all ages and hues, although the difference in reaction between whites and blacks is subtly striking. The African Americans tend to be reserved—quiet pride, knowing nods and be-careful-now looks. The white people, by contrast, are out of control. A nurse named Greta, just off a 12-hour shift, tentatively reaches out to touch the Senator's sleeve. "Oh, my God! Oh, my God! I just touched a future President! I can't believe it!" She is shaking with delight—her voice is quivering—as she asks Obama for an autograph and then a hug.

Indeed, as we traveled that Saturday through downstate Illinois and into the mythic presidential-campaign state of Iowa, Obama seemed the political equivalent of a rainbow—a sudden preternatural event inspiring awe and ecstasy. Bill Gluba, a longtime local Democratic activist, reminisced about driving Bobby Kennedy around Davenport, Iowa, on May 14, 1968. "I was just a teenaged kid," he says. "But I'll never forget the way people reacted to Kennedy. Never seen anything like it since—until this guy." The question of when Obama will run for President is omnipresent. That he will eventually run, and win, is assumed by almost everyone who comes to watch him speak. In Davenport a local reporter asks the question directly: "Are you running for President in 2008?" Obama surprises me by saying he's just thinking about the 2006 election right now, which, in the semiotic dance of presidential politics, is definitely not a no. A few days later, I ask Obama the obvious follow-up question: Will he think about running for President in 2008 when the congressional election is over? "When the election is over and my book tour [for *The Audacity of Hope*] is done, I will think about how I can be most useful to the country and how I can reconcile that with being a good dad and a good husband," he says carefully, and then adds, "I haven't completely decided or unraveled that puzzle yet."

The Obama mania is reminiscent of the Colin Powell mania of September 1995, when the general—another political rainbow—leveraged speculation that he might run for President into book sales of 2.6 million copies for his memoir. Powell and Obama have another thing in common: they are black people who—like Tiger Woods, Oprah Winfrey and Michael Jordan—seem to have an iconic power over the American imagination because they transcend racial stereotypes. "It's all about gratitude," says essayist Shelby Steele, who frequently writes about the psychology of race. "White people are just thrilled when a prominent black person comes along and doesn't rub their noses in racial guilt. White people just go crazy over people like that."

When I asked Obama about this, he began to answer before I finished the question. "There's a core decency to the American people that doesn't get enough attention," he said, sitting in his downtown Chicago office, casually dressed in jeans and a dark blue shirt. "Figures like Oprah, Tiger, Michael Jordan give people a shortcut to express their better instincts. You can be cynical about this. You can say, It's easy to love Oprah. It's harder to embrace the idea of putting more resources into opportunities for young black men—some of whom aren't so lovable. But I don't feel that way. I think it's healthy, a good instinct. I just don't want it to stop with Oprah. I'd rather say, If you feel good about me, there's a whole lot of young men out there who could be me if given the chance."

BUT THAT'S NOT QUITE TRUE. THERE AREN'T VERY MANY PEOPLE—EBONY, IVORY or other—who have Obama's distinctive portfolio of talents, or what he calls his "exotic" family history. He told the story in brilliant, painful detail in his first book, *Dreams from My Father,* which may be the best-written memoir ever produced by an American politician. He is African and American, as opposed to African American, although he certainly endured the casual cruelties of everyday life—in the new book, he speaks of white people mistaking him for a valet-parking attendant—that are visited upon nonwhites in America. "I had to reconcile a lot of different threads growing up—race, class," he told me. "For example, I was going to a fancy prep school, and my mother was on food stamps while she was getting her Ph.D." Obama believes his inability to fit neatly into any group or category explains his relentless efforts to understand and reconcile opposing views. But the tendency is so pronounced that it almost seems an obsessive-compulsive tic. I counted no fewer than 50 instances of excruciatingly judicious on-the-one-hand-on-the-other-handedness in *The Audacity of Hope.* At one point, he considers the historic influence of ideological extremists—that is, people precisely unlike him. "It has not always been the pragmatist, the voice of reason, or the force of compromise, that has created the conditions for liberty," he writes about the antislavery movement of the 19th century. "Knowing this, I can't summarily dismiss those possessed of similar certainty today—the antiabortion activist . . . the animal rights activist who raids a laboratory—no matter how deeply I disagree with their views. I am robbed even of the certainty of uncertainty—for sometimes absolute truths may well be absolute."

Yikes. But then Obama is nothing if not candid about his uncertainties and imperfections. In *The Audacity of Hope,* I counted 28 impolitic or self-deprecating admissions. Immediately, on page 3, he admits to political "restlessness," which is another way of saying he's ambitious. He flays himself for enjoying private jets, which eliminate the cramped frustrations of commercial flying but—on the other hand!—isolate him from the problems of average folks. He concedes that his 2004 Senate opponent, Alan Keyes, got under his skin. He blames himself for "tensions" in his marriage; he doubts his "capacities" as a husband and father.

There is a method to this anguish. Self-deprecation and empathy are powerful political tools. Both those qualities have been integral to Obama's charm from the start. His Harvard Law School classmate Michael Froman told me Obama was elected president of the *Law Review,* the first African American to hold the position, because of his ability to win over the conservatives in their class. "It came down to Barack and a guy named David Goldberg," Froman recalled. "Most of the class were liberals, but there was a growing conservative Federalist Society presence, and there were real fights between right and left about almost every issue. Barack won the election because the conservatives thought he would take their arguments into account."

After three years as a civil rights lawyer and law professor in Chicago, Obama was elected to the Illinois state senate and quickly established himself as different from most of the other African-American legislators. "He was passionate in his views," said Republican state senator Dave Syverson, who worked on welfare reform with Obama. "We had some pretty fierce arguments. But he was not your typical party-line politician. A lot of Democrats didn't want to have any work requirement at all for people on welfare. Barack was willing to make that deal."

THE RAISING AND DASHING OF EXPECTATIONS IS AT THE HEART OF ALMOST every great political drama. In Obama's case, the expectations are ridiculous. He transcends the racial divide so effortlessly that it seems reasonable to expect that he can bridge all the other divisions—and answer all the impossible questions—plaguing American public life. He encourages those expectations by promising great things—at least, in the abstract. "This country is ready for a transformative politics of the sort that John F. Kennedy, Ronald Reagan and Franklin Roosevelt represented," he told me. But those were politicians who had big ideas or were willing to take big risks, and so far, Barack Obama hasn't done much of either. And the annoying truth is, *The Audacity of Hope* isn't very audacious.

I had watched Obama give a speech a few weeks earlier about alternative energy to an audience gathered by MoveOn.org at Georgetown University. It was supposed to be a big deal, a chance for the best-known group of activist Democrats to play footsie with the party's most charismatic speaker. It was a disappointment: Obama proposed a few scraggly carrots and sticks to encourage Detroit to produce more fuel-efficient cars. The audience of students and activists sensed the Senator's timidity and became palpably less enthusiastic as he went on. Just two days before, Al Gore had given a rousing speech in New York City in which he proposed a far more dramatic alternative energy plan: a hefty tax on fossil fuels that would be used, in turn, to reduce Social Security and Medicare taxes. I asked Obama why he didn't support an energy-tax increase married to tax relief for working Americans in the speech or in his book. "I didn't think of it," he replied, but sensing the disingenuousness of his response—talk of a gas tax is everywhere these days—he quickly added, "I think it's a really interesting idea." I pressed him: Had he thought about it? "The premise of this book wasn't to lay out my 10-point plan," he danced. "My goal was to figure out the common values that can serve as a basis for discussion." Sensing my skepticism, he tried again: "This book doesn't drill that deep in terms of policy . . . There are a slew of good ideas out there. Some things end up on the cutting-room floor."

After we jousted over several other issues, Obama felt the need to step back and defend himself. "Look, when I spoke out against going to war in Iraq in 2002, Bush was at 60%-65% in the polls. I was putting my viability as a U.S. Senate candidate at risk. It looks now like an

SHOUT-OUT *From the start, Obama's public appearances, like this one in Detroit, were awe-inspiring events*

easy thing to do, but it wasn't then." He's right: more than a few of his potential rivals for the presidency in 2008 voted to give Bush the authority to use military force in Iraq. Then Obama returned to energy. "When I call for increased fuel-economy standards, that doesn't sit very well with the [United Auto Workers], and they're big buddies of mine . . . Look, it's just not my style to go out of my way to offend people or be controversial just for the sake of being controversial. It makes people feel defensive and more resistant to changes."

Talk about defensive: this was the first time I had seen Obama less than perfectly comfortable. And his discomfort exposed the elaborate intellectual balancing mechanism that he applies to every statement and gesture, to every public moment of his life. "He's working a very dangerous high-wire act," Shelby Steele told me. "He's got to keep on pleasing white folks without offending black folks, and vice versa. You're asking him to take policy risks? Just being who he is is taking an enormous risk."

Back in our interview, I offered Obama a slightly barbed olive branch: maybe my expectations are too high when I ask him to be bold on the issues. "No," he said, and returned again to energy policy—to Gore's tax-swap idea. "It's a neat idea. I'm going to call Gore and have a conversation about it. It might be something I'd want to embrace." But he's not ready to make that leap just yet. Boldness needs to be planned, not blurted—and there are all sorts of questions to ponder before he takes the next step. "In setting your expectations for me now, just remember I haven't announced that I'm running in 2008. I would expect that anyone who's running in 2008, you should have very high expectations for them."

—Originally appeared in TIME, Oct. 23, 2006

Michelle's Gift

*A novelist sets out in search of the real Michelle Obama—
and discovers the appealing down-home values
of America's next First Lady*

BY CURTIS SITTENFELD

MICHELLE OBAMA IS TALL, SMART, FUNNY, RELAXED AND BASICALLY SO glowy and poised—if she's attractive in pictures, she's flat-out gorgeous in person—that it almost seems as if she's already the First Lady. Or at least this is the conclusion I came to after sitting down with her at Denver's Westin Tabor Center during the Democratic National Convention in August. I'd been tagging after her for a couple of days, from one rapturous audience to another, including the crowd at a community-service event for soldiers, at which an Iraq-war veteran introduced her by announcing, "Ma'am, I know you weren't in the military, but I'd follow you anywhere." If all that hadn't quite convinced me (it *was* the Democratic Convention, after all), I'd guess it took roughly the first 30 seconds of our interview for me to fall for her. It happened when I asked whether she gets bored giving the same speech over and over, and she cheerfully replied, "Yeah, absolutely."

It had never been that I didn't like Michelle Obama. (Full disclosure: I voted for Hillary Clinton in Missouri's Democratic primary.) But after writing a novel about a First Lady based

SITTING PRETTY *America's First Lady–in-waiting survived slurs and attacks from talk radio and the right-wing blogosphere*

loosely on Laura Bush, I saw Michelle as, well, controversial. Back in June, when she made a visit to *The View* to talk about policy issues such as panty hose, the appearance was widely considered part of a charm offensive intended to rehabilitate an image damaged by, among other things, the now infamous remark she'd made during a speech a few months before: "For the first time in my adult life, I am proud of my country because it feels like hope is finally making a comeback." I also knew that some people found Michelle to be variously "mean," "uppity" and "radical"—not me, mind you, but people. But when I started asking around, I encountered more Americans who, if anything, seemed more infatuated by Michelle than by her husband—including the white woman I know who bought her first-ever issue of *Ebony* because Michelle was on the cover, and the cameraman I met in Denver who finagled a fist bump with Michelle and then proclaimed that he would never wash his hands again. He assured me he was usually jaded in these kinds of situations, but Michelle was the second coming of Jackie O.!

During our interview, I asked Michelle what accounts for the discrepancy between the admiration she inspires and the kind of blogosphere and talk-radio slurs that prompted the *New Yorker,* even if in jest, to run its notorious cover cartoon of her standing with her husband in the Oval Office, sporting an Afro and an AK-47. "I've realized that there are two conversations that go on," she said. "There's one at the punditry level—the polls, the writers, the folks in the know, they have one set of conversations—and then there's what's happening on the ground. Early on, I learned to base my reactions on what I see on the ground, because that to me is a more accurate reflection—even, as it turned out, in the primary. If you read the papers, you wouldn't have predicted the outcome of Iowa [where Obama was victorious in the 2008 caucus]. But if you were in Iowa, you could feel the clear possibility of what the outcome would be."

My own theory is that the media, bolstered by conservative wishful thinking, got bored with the early Michelle Obama narrative—that she was a successful professional with a blue collar background, degrees from Princeton and Harvard, and a penchant for making wifely jabs about her husband's morning breath—and switched to the Michelle-as-liability narrative to keep things entertaining. Certainly it seems that Michelle has paid as steep a political price for her national-pride remark, which some of us were not actually offended by, as Cindy McCain has for any of her own shortcomings.

The delicate dance that Michelle is required to perform calls to mind the axiom that blacks must be twice as good as whites to get half as far. A few Democrats—and feminists—expressed disappointment at her convention speech, with its subtext of, Ignore my race and my Ivy League education and look how warm and maternal and unthreatening I am. But others, including, presumably, Michelle herself, recognized this soft approach as a necessity.

The most poignant comment I heard her make during the days I followed her was one she shared with a group of five female newspaper columnists. As a professional black woman who grew up in a stable family and now has a stable family of her own, she told the columnists, "Sometimes I do feel as if people don't believe I exist. I'm probably the first person of my kind the nation has seen out there." Or, as Whoopi Goldberg put it during Michelle's June appearance on *The View,* "I have to say I'm really glad to see you because . . . any time you see black folks on the news, particularly women, they have no teeth, and the teeth that they have have gold around them, and they can't put a sentence together."

When we talked, I wondered whether it really should be Michelle's responsibility to refute such biases. Michelle replied that she's used to it. "That has been my experience my whole life," she said. "That's why education is so important. That's why giving all kids a chance to go away to college is important. We grow up in our communities and our neighborhoods and our families, and we know what we know. It's no fault. It's no blame. But when people have a chance to interact and have conversations—you don't even have to live under the same roof. There are many people who went to college with me who got to see me and know me, and whether [or not] they knew me personally, they took away the experience. That's the nature of life when you're in the minority in most situations . . . I feel like that's a role that I should play."

T HE FACT THAT SHE HAS PLAYED IT FOR SO LONG HELPS TO EXPLAIN THE APPARent ease with which she has handled the intensity of the campaign. "When you're a person like me, who steps outside the normal boundaries of what their life is supposed to be like—say, going to Princeton—you're worried that maybe you're not prepared, because everybody has told you you probably won't be, and then you get there and you're like, I'm prepared." She laughed. "I think many of us are more prepared for certain situations than we imagine."

If the campaign had its rough patches, what's surprising is how unguarded Michelle still seems: the most endearing and entertaining parts of her public appearances are ad-libbed, whether she's bragging to a Denver audience that she's wearing sensible shoes or she's referring to Barack as "this guy that I know, this man that I married," before mischievously adding, "his cute self." Anyone who doubts her off-the-cuff charm should Google the clip in which she's giving an outdoor speech and her dress flies up in the wind. Deftly catching it, she tells the audience, "I don't mean to flash you guys . . . I'm not going to be on YouTube."

And this is Michelle Obama's greatest gift: her ability to relate to regular people, and vice versa. Even though she's taller and fitter and better educated than most of us, she is completely and totally believable as a person who lives in the same world we do, who consumes the same pop culture (*Us Weekly,* anyone?) and shops at the same stores (Target, Gap) and struggles with most if not all of the same personal and professional juggling acts.

Few political spouses in recent memory, and even fewer First Ladies, have seemed this familiar. Take, for example, Laura Bush. I'm a fan of hers, in large part because she comes across as a truly kind, decent person. Her combination of intellectual curiosity and total discretion intrigues me. But if Laura inspires my affection and sympathy, I don't exactly relate to her. She is of an older generation and has made choices, like quitting her job after getting married but before having children, that are the choices of another time. Michelle Obama, by contrast, had a higher income than her husband for part of their marriage.

And contrary to her claims, Michelle is not the first person of her kind I've seen; she's actually recognizable as a very particular type, though it took me until after the convention to figure out what that type is. I suspect this person will be familiar to anyone who has, in the past 25 years, been a young, college-educated woman in her first real job: where there's a woman eight or 10 years older than you who's not only visibly good at what she does but also confident and friendly and busy with a life that features a cute husband and a nice house and maybe even a couple of kids. And you think maybe, if everything goes right, your own life could turn out like hers.

—Originally appeared in TIME, Oct. 6, 2008

JUNE 3, 2008
LOOKING LIKE A WINNER

Obama rides an elevator to a victory rally at the Xcel arena in St. Paul, Minn., having just earned enough support from delegates and superdelegates to clinch the nomination

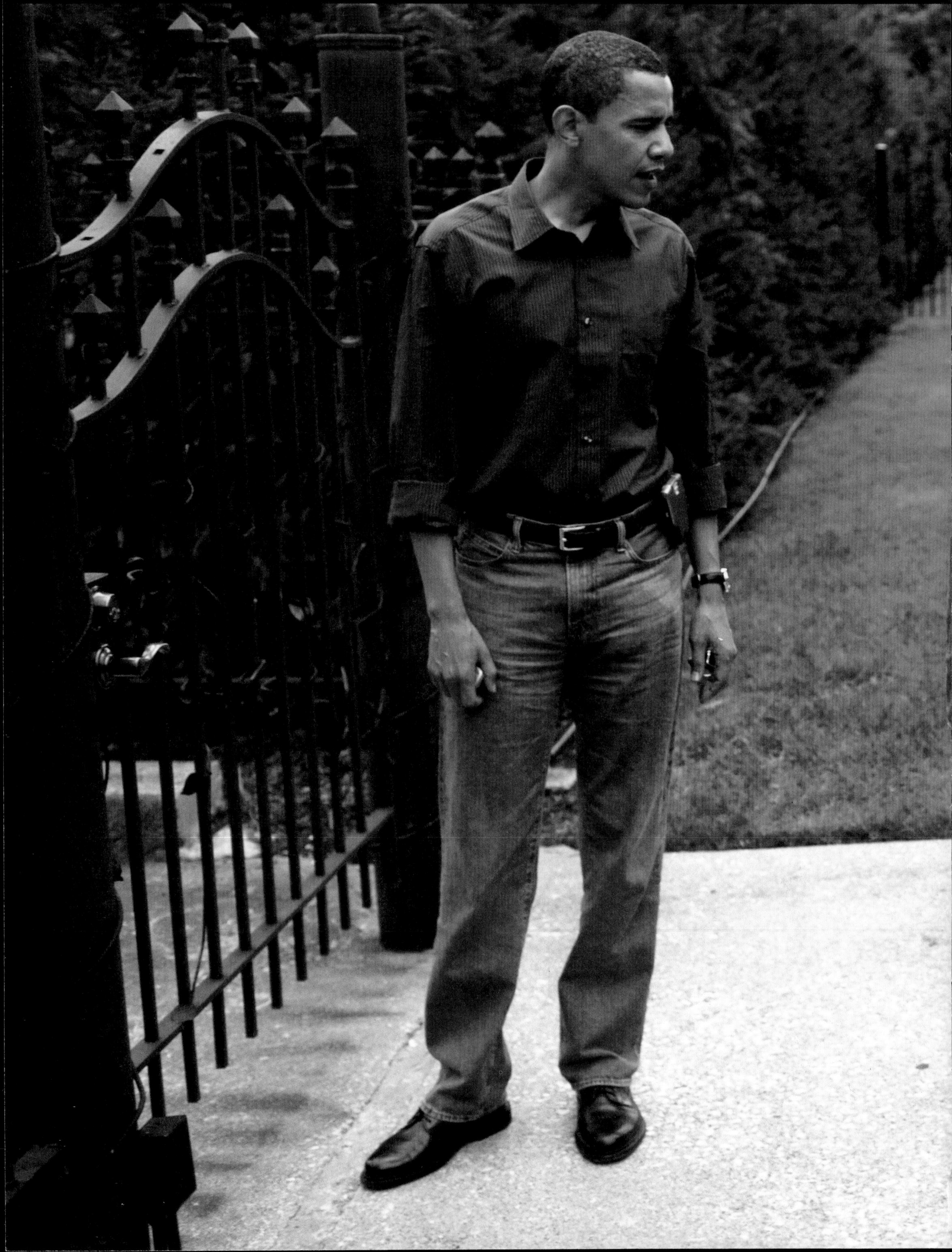

Oct. 2, 2008
JUST ANOTHER DAD

*Looking casual, Obama spends a rare morning
relaxing at home in Chicago's Hyde Park, taking
daughters Malia, left, and Sasha to school*

JAN. 21, 2008
YOUNG DREAMERS

*Before a Martin Luther King Jr. Day event in
Columbia, S.C., two youthful supporters fix
their gaze on Obama as he works the crowd*

RIZ

APRIL 5, 2008
COMPETITIVE STREAK

*Not to be outdone by two aides who each did a pair
of pull-ups, Obama does three before stepping out to
address the crowd at the University of Montana*

NOV. 2, 2007
BREAKING THROUGH

*In Manning, S.C., a crowd watches Obama speak outside
a courthouse. He worked hard at that stage to convince
skeptical black voters that he could actually win.*

After accepting the Democratic nomination,
Obama leads his family out to face the cheering
crowd at Invesco Field in Denver

A Mother's Story

Obama's greatest influence was a woman
most Americans know nothing about. How his mother's
uncommon life shaped his views of the world

BY AMANDA RIPLEY

E ACH OF US LIVES A LIFE OF CONTRADICTORY TRUTHS. WE ARE NOT ONE THING or another. Barack Obama's mother was at least a dozen things. S. Ann Soetoro was a teen mother who later got a Ph.D. in anthropology; a white woman from the Midwest who was more comfortable in Indonesia; a natural-born mother obsessed with her work; a romantic pragmatist, if such a thing is possible. "When I think about my mother," Obama told me, "I think that there was a certain combination of being very grounded in who she was, what she believed in. But also a certain recklessness. I think she was always searching for something. She wasn't comfortable seeing her life confined to a certain box."

Obama's mother was a dreamer. She made risky bets that paid off only some of the time, choices that her children had to live with. She fell in love—twice—with fellow students from distant countries she knew nothing about. Both marriages failed, and she leaned on her parents and friends to help raise her two children. "She cried a lot," said her daughter Maya Soetoro-Ng, "if she saw animals being treated cruelly or children in the news or a sad movie—or if she

HERITAGE *Obama's mother, with her parents, top right, in Kansas in the mid-'40s, transcended her middle-class, Midwest, midcentury upbringing to become a capable single mother and fearless champion of the underprivileged in Indonesia. Obama, with his mother, left, in Hawaii in 1962 and around age 6, above, inherited her penetrating mind and her fearlessness. Obama's charismatic father Barack Sr., above middle, left his son when he was a year old, returning for just one visit before his death in 1982*

felt like she wasn't being understood in a conversation." And yet she was fearless, said Soetoro-Ng. "She was very capable. She went out on the back of a motorcycle and did rigorous fieldwork. She saw the heart of a problem, and she knew whom to hold accountable."

Obama is partly a product of what his mother was not. Whereas she swept her children off to unfamiliar lands and even lived apart from her son when he was a teenager, Obama has tried to ground his family in the Midwest. "We've created stability for our kids in a way that my mom didn't do for us," he said. "My choosing to put down roots in Chicago and marry a woman who is very rooted in one place probably indicates a desire for stability that maybe I was missing."

Ironically, the person who mattered most in Obama's life is the one we know the least about—maybe because being partly African in America is still seen as being simply black, and color is still a preoccupation above all else. There is not enough room in the conversation for the rest of a man's story. But Obama is his mother's son. In his wide-open rhetoric about what can be instead of what was, you see a hint of his mother's credulity. When he got donations from people who had never believed in politics before, they were responding to his ability—passed down from his mother—to make a powerful argument without using a trace of ideology. On a good day, when he figures out how to move a crowd of people very different from himself, it probably helps to have had a parent who gazed at different cultures the way other people study gems.

BORN IN 1942, OBAMA'S MOTHER, STANLEY ANN DUNHAM, CAME INTO AN AMERica constrained by war, segregation and a distrust of difference. Her parents named her Stanley because her father, a furniture salesman, had wanted a boy. She spent her high school years, after having moved at least five times—to towns in Kansas, California, Texas and Washington—on an island near Seattle, taking advanced classes in philosophy. "She was a very intelligent, quiet girl," recalled Maxine Box, a high school friend. "She wasn't particularly interested in children or in getting married." After she finished high school, her father whisked the family away again—this time to Honolulu, part of the new state of Hawaii, after he heard about a big new furniture store there. Stanley grudgingly went along yet again, enrolling in the University of Hawaii.

Just before moving to Hawaii, she saw her first foreign film, *Black Orpheus,* a sentimental—to some eyes, patronizing—tale of doomed love, filmed in Brazil. Years later Obama saw it with his mother and thought about walking out. But looking at her in the theater, he glimpsed her 16-year-old self. "I suddenly realized," he wrote in his memoir, *Dreams from My Father,* "that the depiction of childlike blacks I was now seeing on the screen . . . was what my mother had carried with her to Hawaii all those years before, a reflection of the simple fantasies that had been forbidden to a white middle-class girl from Kansas, the promise of another life, warm, sensual, exotic, different."

By college, Stanley had started introducing herself as Ann. She met Barack Obama Sr. in a Russian-language class. He was one of the first Africans to attend the University of Hawaii and a focus of great curiosity. "He had this magnetic personality," remembered Neil Abercrombie, a member of Congress from Hawaii who was friends with Obama Sr. in college. "Everything was oratory from him, even the most commonplace observation."

Obama's father quickly drew a crowd of friends at the university. "We would drink beer, eat pizza and play records," Abercrombie said. They talked about Vietnam and politics. "Everyone had an opinion, and everyone was of the opinion that everyone wanted to hear their opinion—no one more so than Barack." The exception was Ann, the quiet young woman in the corner. Obama Sr.'s friends knew he was dating a white woman, but they made a point of treating it as a nonissue. This was Hawaii, after all, a place renowned as a melting pot.

On Feb. 2, 1961, several months after they met, Obama's parents got married in Maui. At that point, Ann was three months pregnant with Barack Obama II. Friends did not learn of the wedding until afterward. The motivations behind the marriage remain a mystery, even to Obama. "I never probed my mother about the details. Did they decide to get married because she was already pregnant? Or did he propose to her in the traditional, formal way?" Obama wondered. "I suppose, had she not passed away, I would have asked more."

When Obama was almost 1, his father left for Harvard to get a Ph.D. in economics. He had an agenda: to return to Kenya and help reinvent it. He wanted to take his new family with him. But he also had a wife from a previous marriage there. In the end, Ann decided not to follow him. "She was under no illusions," said Abercrombie. "He was a man of his time, from a very patriarchal society." Ann filed for divorce in Honolulu in January 1964, citing "grievous mental suffering"—the reason given in most divorces at the time.

Ann had already done things most women of her generation had not: she had married an African, had their baby and gotten divorced. At this juncture, her life could have become narrower—a marginalized woman focused on raising a child on her own. She could have filled her son's head with well-founded resentment for his absent father. But that is not what happened.

When her son was almost 2, Ann returned to college. Money was tight. She collected food stamps and relied on her parents to help take care of young Barack. At school, she met another foreign student, Lolo Soetoro. He was easygoing, happily playing with her young son. Lolo proposed in 1967. When mother and son later joined Lolo in Indonesia, it was the first time either had left the country. "Walking off the plane, the tarmac rippling with heat, the sun bright as a furnace," Obama later remembered, "I clutched her hand, determined to protect her."

Lolo's house on the outskirts of Jakarta was a long way from the high-rises of Honolulu. There was no electricity, and the streets were not paved. Ann and her son were the first foreigners to live in the neighborhood, according to locals who remember them. Two baby crocodiles, along with chickens and birds of paradise, occupied the backyard. To get to know the kids next door, Obama sat on the wall between their houses and flapped his arms like a great, big bird, making cawing noises, recalled Kay Ikranagara, a friend. "That got the kids laughing." Obama attended a Catholic school, Franciscus Assisi Primary. He attracted attention since he was not only a foreigner but also chubbier than the locals. But he seemed to shrug off the teasing, eating tofu and tempeh like all the other kids, playing soccer and picking guavas from the trees.

As Ann became more intrigued by Indonesia, her husband became more Western. He rose through the ranks of an American oil company and moved the family to a nicer neighborhood. She was bored by the dinner parties he took her to, where men boasted about golf scores and wives complained about their Indonesian servants. "She wasn't prepared for the loneliness," Obama wrote in *Dreams*. "It was constant, like a shortness of breath." And while Indonesia has the world's largest Muslim population, Obama's household was not religious. "My mother . . . was one of the most spiritual souls I ever knew," Obama said in a 2007 speech. "But she had a healthy skepticism of religion as an institution. And as a consequence, so did I."

Ann took a job teaching English at the U.S. embassy. She went into her son's room every day at 4 a.m. to give him English lessons from a U.S. correspondence course. After two years at the Catholic school, Obama moved to a state-run elementary school closer to the new house. He was the only foreigner, said Ati Kisjanto, a classmate. At night, to compensate for the absence of black people in her son's life, Ann brought home books on the civil rights movement and recordings of Mahalia Jackson. Her aspirations for racial harmony were simplistic. "She believed that people were all basically the same under their skin," Obama said, "that bigotry of any sort was wrong and that the goal was then to treat everybody as unique individuals."

In 1971, when Obama was 10, Ann sent him back to Hawaii to live with her parents and attend Punahou, an élite prep school that he'd gotten into on a scholarship. The wrenching decision seemed to reflect how much she valued education. Obama, in his book, described an adolescence shadowed by a sense of alienation. "I didn't feel [her absence] as a deprivation," Obama told me. "But when I think about the fact that I was separated from her, I suspect it had more of an impact than I know." A year later, Ann followed Obama back to Hawaii, taking her daughter but leaving her husband behind. She enrolled in a master's program to study the anthropology of Indonesia. She began to find her voice. People who knew her before describe her as quiet and smart; those who met her afterward use words like *forthright* and *passionate*. Ann's husband visited Hawaii frequently, but they never lived together again. (She filed for divorce in 1980.) Three years after coming back to Hawaii, she returned to Indonesia to do fieldwork for her Ph.D. Obama, then about 14, told her he would stay behind. He was tired of being new.

IN INDONESIA, ANN JOKED TO FRIENDS THAT HER SON SEEMED INTERESTED ONLY IN basketball. "She despaired of him ever having a social conscience," recalled Richard Patten, a colleague. She took a job at the Ford Foundation and spent a lot of time with villagers, learning their priorities and problems. Her home became a gathering spot for the powerful and the marginalized: politicians, filmmakers, musicians and labor organizers. She cared deeply about helping poor women. "She spoke mostly in positive terms: what we are trying to do and what we can do," said her daughter. "She wasn't ideological," said Obama. "I inherited that, I think, from her."

While his mother was helping poor people in Indonesia, Obama was trying to do something similar 7,000 miles away in Chicago as a community organizer. Ann's friends say she was delighted by his career move and started every conversation with an update of her children's lives. "All of us knew how brilliant he was," remembered Ann's friend Georgia McCauley.

In the fall of 1994, Ann was having dinner at a friend's house in Jakarta when she felt a pain in her stomach. A local doctor diagnosed indigestion. When Ann returned to Hawaii several months later, she learned it was ovarian and uterine cancer. She died on Nov. 7, 1995, at 52.

Before her death, Ann read a draft of her son's memoir, which is almost entirely about his father. People who knew her say she didn't seem bothered. "She just said it was something he had to work out," said Nancy Peluso, a friend. Neither Ann nor her son knew how little time they had left, and Obama has said his biggest mistake was not being at her side when she died. He went to Hawaii to help the family scatter the ashes over the Pacific. And he surely carries on her spirit. "When Barack smiles," said Peluso, "there's just a certain *Ann* look. He lights up in a particular way that she did." —WITH REPORTING BY ZAMIRA LOEBIS AND JASON TEDJASUKMANA

—Originally appeared in TIME, April 21, 2008

ABOUT A BOY *Obama's grandparents (that's grandfather Stanley Dunham with Obama at the beach, top left) helped raise him, trying, despite his father's absence and tight family finances, to give him an idyllic Hawaiian upbringing that included tricycling, top right, and swimming, middle right. Obama's mother's marriage to Lolo Soetoro, an Indonesian businessman (their 1968 family picture, above, includes Barack's half sister Maya) eventually fell apart. Obama's father, at right with his 10-year-old son during his month-long return to Hawaii in 1971, encouraged Barack to study and shared tales of his Kenyan origins*

How He
Learned to Win

*Trounced in his first big race, Obama retooled and won a
Senate seat. How the ward politics in Chicago gave him an
education that would earn him the presidency*

BY MICHAEL WEISSKOPF

BARACK OBAMA HAD NOT BEEN IN POLITICS FOR LONG WHEN HE GOT HIS TAIL
whipped by a veteran Chicago Congressman in his own backyard in 2000. For
a brief period that followed, Obama seemed a bit unsure about what to do with
his life. Yet within four years, Obama had won a seat in the U.S. Senate. And
just four years after that, he has been elected President.

How did Obama come so far so fast? Much of the answer can be traced
to the lessons of that first thumping. It was after that race, aides and associates say, that Obama
learned how to be a politician. He jettisoned his Harvard-tested speaking style for something
more down-home. He learned how to cultivate those in power without being defined by them.
And he learned how to be different things to different people: a reformer groomed by an old-
fashioned machine boss, a Harvard lawyer whose bootstrapping life story gained traction with
white ethnics. Abner Mikva, a former federal judge and Congressman from Chicago, says
Obama figured out "how to appeal to different constituencies without being inconsistent."

In the midcentury heyday of Chicago's Democratic machine, politics was open only to

FIRST HAND *During early campaigns, like this run for state senate in the mid-'90s, Obama began to refine his tone and approach*

those with a sponsor—"We don't want nobody nobody sent," a ward boss famously said. It was no longer so exclusive by the time Obama got into the game. The centrally controlled party organization had splintered into a loose group of ward committees that operated like autonomous fiefs. But old practices died hard: loyalty and familiarity were rewarded by new bosses who expected newcomers to pay their dues—and wait their turn. One exception was Hyde Park, a small, integrated neighborhood of professionals, with a long tradition of independent politics. Obama moved there as a newly minted lawyer, and in 1996 he won his first political election, to represent Hyde Park in the state senate. After three years in the state capital of Springfield, already restless, he began to eye the seat for the First Congressional District of Illinois.

The First had the longest continuous black representation of any district in Congress. Since 1992, it had been represented by Bobby Rush, who had co-founded the Illinois Black Panther Party before going mainstream as an alderman and ward committeeman. But Rush stumbled badly in 1999 when he took on incumbent Richard M. Daley in the mayoral primary, losing even his own south-side ward. His misstep made Obama think he could take Rush on.

During the campaign, Obama argued that Rush had failed as a leader. But his delivery was stiff, professorial—"more Harvard than Chicago," said an adviser who had watched Obama put a church audience to sleep. The problem was deeper than speaking style. Obama was a cultural outsider. "He went to Harvard and became an educated fool," Rush said. Not growing up on the South Side raised suspicions. So did his white mother and Establishment manner. Obama's first encounter with racial politics was over the perception that he wasn't black enough. "Barack is viewed in part to be the white man in blackface," state senator Donne Trotter said at the time.

It didn't help Obama that he missed a crucial state senate vote on gun control and that President Bill Clinton publicly endorsed Rush. In the end, Rush racked up 61% of the vote, compared with 30% for Obama. Obama lost the heavily black wards by 4 to 1. "I confess to you," he told about 50 supporters on that chilly March election night, "winning is better than losing."

T HE CAMPAIGN LEFT OBAMA $60,000 IN DEBT AND UNSURE OF HIS FUTURE. From the ashes, though, Obama, then 38, saw a way out. The only ward he had won was the 19th, largely white working-class and Irish Catholic, suggesting a wider reach among white voters. But if Obama was going to make the leap, he would need the help of men like Emil Jones. A former sewer inspector in Chicago, the wheeling-and-dealing African-American Jones worked his way up the Democratic machine to become Illinois's senate president in 2003. Early that year, he met privately with Obama at the statehouse. Obama had found a race to his liking: the U.S. Senate seat held by a Republican up for re-election in 2004. If Obama were to have any hope, he would have to overcome two weaknesses exposed in 2000: shaky support among working-class blacks and the dearth of party regulars. Jones held the key to both problems. "You," Obama told him, "have the power to make a United States Senator." Jones heard Obama out and then told him, "Let's go for it."

By embracing Obama early, Jones stopped pivotal endorsements of rivals. Candidate Blair Hull, who made a fortune in securities trading, had a claim on the support of Governor Rod Blagojevich, whose 2002 victory Hull had helped underwrite. But, as Jones put it, "the governor needs support for his initiatives, so naturally he's not going to take a chance at alienating me." Blagojevich stayed neutral. Illinois comptroller Dan Hynes was the presumptive favorite, the son of a former state senate president and close Daley ally. The AFL-CIO was gearing up for an early endorsement of the younger Hynes. Jones called its president. "If you proceed in that direction, you lose me," Jones told her. The union backed off, giving him and Obama time to line up support from affiliates that had large and heavily black memberships.

With Hull and Hynes likely to split the white vote, Obama would need blanket support from African Americans. In seven years in Springfield, Obama was best known for passing ethics reform, not social-justice legislation. But Jones now controlled the body and picked Obama to steer (and get credit for) laws that passed after years of demands by the black community: death-penalty reform, fatter tax credits for the working poor, a measure to curb racial profiling.

Obama, meanwhile, junked his starchy speaking style. Dan Shomon, his campaign manager against Rush, believes Obama learned the art of public speaking at the scores of black churches he visited in 2000, absorbing the rhythm and flourishes of pastors and watching how their congregations reacted. He emphasized his Christian faith and often mentioned his own pastor, Jeremiah Wright, who would become an election-year lightning rod. And he drew from other parts of his life story to broaden support among whites. His rise from a modest upbringing to the pinnacle of U.S. education drew a connection to the life struggles of ordinary people.

And while Obama couldn't win the support of the Daleys' political machine—he knew it would back Hynes—he shrewdly planted some political seeds. He wrote Bill Daley, a longtime Democratic wise man, saying that while it was only right for the Daleys to support a loyal friend, he hoped they would be for him if he won the primary. "I thought, That's a very smooth move," said the younger Daley, who this year supported Obama for the White House.

Obama was politicking at a high level and building an organization to pay for it. In the 2000 loss, Obama had raised $600,000, an eye-popping figure for a first-time congressional candidate. He now laid down a challenge to Marty Nesbitt, a top fund raiser. "If you raise $4 million, I have a 40% chance of winning," Nesbitt recalled him saying. "If you raise $10 million, I guarantee you I can win." Said Nesbitt: "It was a matter of having the money to tell his story."

Obama had already opened a rich vein of political cash in Chicago's black business élite. He put flamboyant Chicago real estate tycoon Tony Rezko on his finance committee. But to raise $10 million, he would have to win over Chicago's biggest political donors, who mostly had had no personal contact with him. Many of them did, however, know his black inner circle. Nesbitt was close to Penny Pritzker of the Hyatt hotel clan and told her of Obama's Senate plans. Pritzker was initially skeptical—"Didn't he just lose a congressional race to Bobby Rush?"—but agreed to hear Obama out. On a weekend at her Michigan summer home, he won her over, landing an ally whose Rolodex contained the names of Chicago's leading business, cultural, Jewish and philanthropic figures, helping him to raise almost $6 million in the primary.

Obama's lunge for high office would not prove much of a contest. His Democratic rivals tore each other up, letting Obama mostly keep to the high road. The Senate race turned into a rout, with Obama taking nearly 53% of the vote in a three-way contest. Obama went on to crush the Republican, Alan Keyes, winning the seat. The seeds of Obama's political future were planted during that primary campaign. At his primary victory party in May 2004, he noted the improbable triumph of a "skinny guy from the South Side with a funny name like Barack Obama." Then he repeated a line that had capped his campaign commercials: "Yes, we can."

—Originally appeared in TIME, May 19, 2008

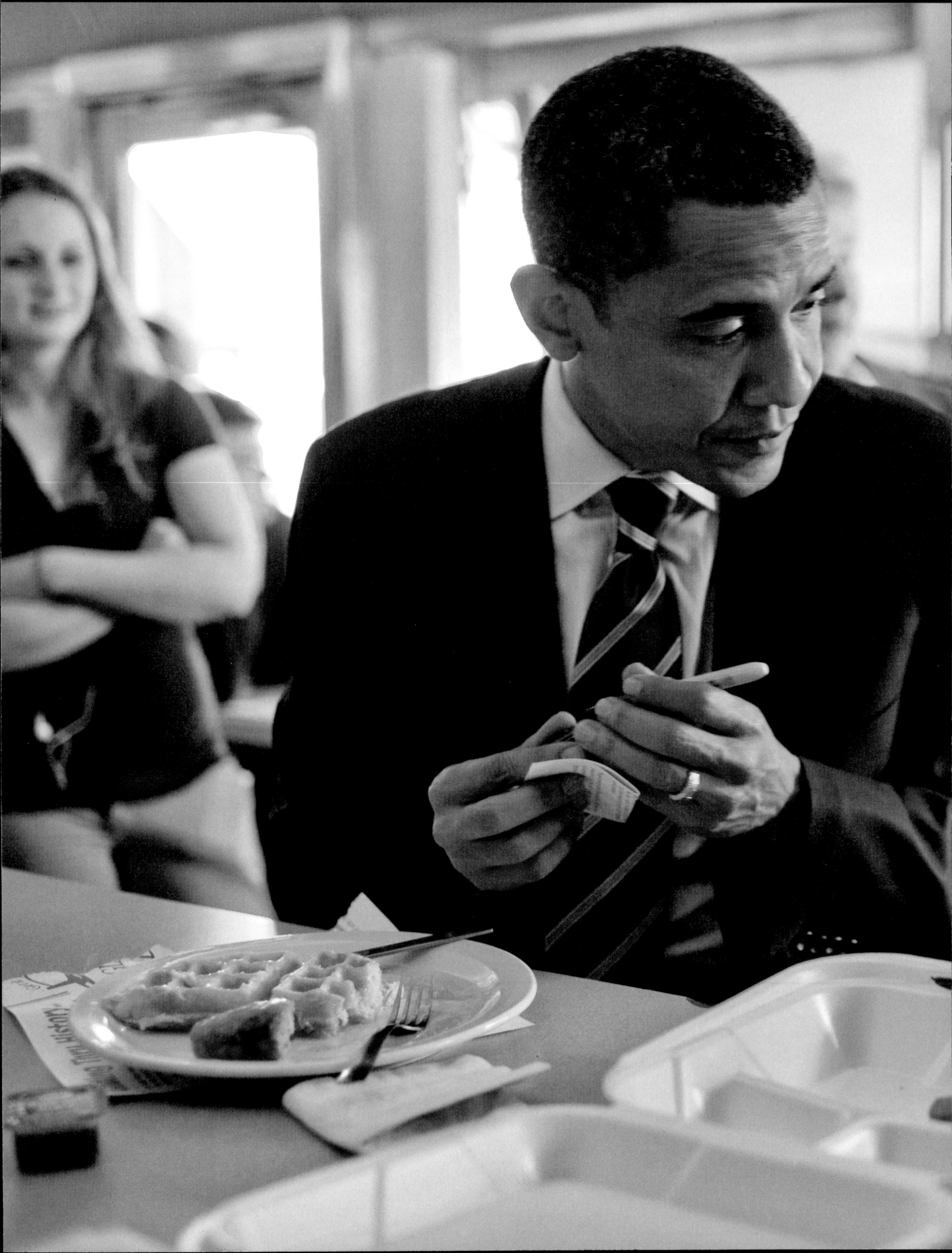

JULY 4, 2008
HOOPING IT UP

Even at the height of the campaign,
there were moments of levity, as at this
Independence Day picnic in Butte, Mont.

APRIL 19, 2008
SIGNING BONUS

During a daylong train tour of Pennsylvania,
Obama takes a moment to autograph copies of his
books at the Lancaster train station

JUNE 3, 2008
WE DID IT

Having all but secured the Democratic nomination,
Obama shares a moment with Michelle before
facing the crowd at the Xcel arena in St. Paul, Minn.

Oct. 18, 2008
THEY WANT CHANGE

*Obama waves to some of the 100,000 people who turned out to
hear him speak at a rally under the Gateway Arch in St. Louis, Mo.
It was his largest crowd at a U.S. event while campaigning*

CHANGE
WE CAN
BELIEVE IN
BarackObama.com

JAN. 6, 2008
REST FOR THE WEARY

In the middle of a long day of events in
New Hampshire, Obama grabs a quick nap on
his campaign bus as he heads to another rally

A Star Is Born

At the Democratic Convention in 2004, Obama introduced himself to the nation and dazzled viewers with a passionate, hope-filled speech about "one America"

BY AMY SULLIVAN

POLITICAL CAREERS HAD BEEN LAUNCHED AT CONVENTIONS BEFORE. HUBERT Humphrey was the mayor of Minneapolis in 1948 when he urged Democrats at their convention to embrace the cause of civil rights. Ronald Reagan was still an actor when he electrified the 1964 GOP Convention with a nominating speech for Barry Goldwater. But it would be 20 years before Humphrey became his party's presidential nominee, and 16 before Reagan became his party's choice. And then there was The Speech—Barack Obama's 2004 address to the Democratic Convention in Boston that propelled a political trajectory almost directly to the White House.

Obama was a state senator when he addressed the convention. At the 2000 gathering, he hadn't even rated a credential from Illinois's delegation. Yet in 2004, Mary Beth Cahill, John Kerry's campaign manager, selected him to deliver the keynote address. She needed someone who could energize voters, and at a gig with Kerry in Chicago that spring, Obama had stolen the show.

He delivered the speech of his life. Obama was impressively loose in his first national appearance, riding the applause and ad-libbing as if he'd done it many times before. And he showed precocious speechwriting skill. Knowing that most viewers hadn't heard of him, Obama artfully sketched out his complex personal story. He conveyed love for his family, but when he noted that both of his parents had died, he seemed to be presenting himself both as an orphan and as a child of America. "In no other country on earth," he said, "is my story even possible."

Having established how a "skinny kid with a funny name" could relate to Americans from

SHOWSTOPPER *Obama laid out an optimistic vision for America and dared fellow citizens to be so audacious*

all walks of life, Obama then spoke about the roles of individuals and of the state in fixing society. Government has responsibilities, he argued, but so do parents and communities: "Parents have to parent . . . children can't achieve unless we raise their expectations and turn off the televisions sets and eradicate the slander that says a black youth with a book is acting white." It was a powerful message, particularly from a black politician, and it established for white listeners that Obama was not from the strident, divisive school of politics of Jesse Jackson or Al Sharpton.

He spoke passionately about "one America." Although the idea of "two Americas" was a defining argument of the Kerry-Edwards campaign, Obama presented a more positive, united view. It was one part communitarian—"I am my brother's keeper; I am my sister's keeper"—and one part rebuke of ideologues on the right and the left. "There's not a liberal America and a conservative America," insisted Obama. "There's the United States of America."

He brought it all home with a message of resounding optimism, asking the crowd, "Do we participate in a politics of cynicism or a politics of hope?" "Hope!" they shouted back. Hope, he concluded, "is God's greatest gift to us, the bedrock of this nation; the belief in things not seen, the belief that there are better days ahead."

Obama was testing the country's capacity for audacity. And it worked. Throughout the 2008 campaign, supporters across the nation pointed to that evening as the moment when they decided to get behind this guy whose name they couldn't yet pronounce. On Nov. 4, a majority of Americans cast their lot with hope.

Defeating Hillary

*By building a new political machine, Obama became the first
insurgent Democrat in decades to dethrone a front runner.
In an exclusive interview, he described his path to a historic victory*

By Karen Tumulty

BARACK OBAMA WAS CAMPAIGNING IN SOUTH CAROLINA IN OCTOBER 2007 when he got an urgent call from Penny Pritzker, the hotel mogul who led his campaign's finance committee. About 200 of his biggest fund raisers were meeting in Des Moines, Iowa, and among them, near panic was setting in. Pritzker's team had raised money faster than any other campaign ever had. Its candidate was drawing mega-crowds wherever he went. Yet he was still running at least 20 points behind Hillary Clinton in polls. His above-the-fray brand of politics just wasn't getting the job done, and some of his top moneymen were urging him to rethink his strategy, shake up his staff, go negative. You'd better get here, Pritzker told Obama. And fast.

Obama made an unscheduled appearance that Sunday night and called for a show of hands from his finance committee. "Can I see how many people in this room I told that this was going to be easy?" he asked. "If anybody signed up thinking it was going to be easy, then I didn't make myself clear." A win in the Iowa caucus in January, Obama promised, would give him the momentum he needed to win across the map—but his backers wouldn't see much

THE PATH TO VICTORY *Two months before the key Iowa caucus, Obama met with residents of Burlington to explain his vision for America*

evidence of progress before then. "We're up against the most formidable team in 25 years," he said. "But we've got a plan, and we've got to have faith in it."

That faith was rewarded. The 2008 presidential campaign produced its share of surprises, but one of the most important was that a newcomer from Chicago put together by far the best political operation of either party. Obama's campaign was that rare, frictionless machine that ran with the energy of an insurgency and the efficiency of a corporation. His team lacked what his rivals' specialized in: there were no staff shake-ups, no financial crises, no changes in game plan and no visible strife. Even its campaign slogan—"Change we can believe in"—would survive the entire contest.

How did he do it? How did Obama become the first Democratic insurgent in a generation or more to knock off the party's Establishment front runner? Facing an operation as formidable as Clinton's, Obama said in a June interview, "was liberating . . . What I'd felt was that we could try some things in a different way and build an organization that reflected my personality and what I thought the country was looking for. We didn't have to unlearn a bunch of bad habits."

When Betsy Myers first met with Obama in his Senate office on Jan. 3, 2007, about two weeks before he announced he was forming an exploratory committee to run for President, Obama laid down three ruling principles for his future chief operating officer: Run the campaign with respect; build it from the bottom up; and finally, no drama. Myers was struck by how closely Obama had studied the two campaigns of George W. Bush. "He said he wanted to run our campaign like a business," said Myers. And in a good business, the customer is king. Early on, before it had the resources to do much else, the campaign outsourced a "customer-service center" so that anyone who called, at any hour of the day or night, would find a human voice on the other end of the line.

Meanwhile, Obama's Chicago headquarters made technology its running mate from the start. That wasn't just for fund-raising: in state after state, the campaign turned over its voter lists—normally a closely guarded crown jewel—to volunteers, who used their own laptops and the unlimited night and weekend minutes of their cell-phone plans to contact every name and populate a political organization from the ground up. "The tools were there, and they built it," said Joe Trippi, who ran Howard Dean's 2004 campaign. "In a lot of ways, the Dean campaign was like the Wright brothers. Four years later, we're watching the Apollo project."

Even Obama concedes he did not expect the Internet to be such a good friend. "What I didn't anticipate was how effectively we could use the Internet to harness that grass-roots base, both on the financial side and the organizing side," Obama said. "That, I think, was probably one of the biggest surprises of the campaign, just how powerfully our message merged with the social networking and the power of the Internet." But three other fundamentals were crucial to making Obama the Democratic nominee:

A Brave New Party

In most elections, the Iowa caucuses are an anomaly. Competing there is a complicated, labor-intensive undertaking that, once finished, is cast off as an oddity and never repeated. But in 2008 it became for Obama the road test of a youth-oriented, technology-fueled organization and the model for many of the wins that followed. It was also a challenge to history. The iron rule of Iowa had always been that caucusgoers tended to look the same year in and year out: older people, union households, party stalwarts—the kind of folks who would seem more inclined to back Clinton or John Edwards—trudging out into the cold night for a few hours of political conversation. Instead, Obama saw Iowa as a chance to put a stake through Clinton's inevitability. "Mission No. 1 was finishing ahead of Hillary Clinton in Iowa," recalled Obama campaign manager David Plouffe. "If we hadn't done that, it would have been hard to stop her."

But counting on new voters had proved disastrous for Dean in 2004. The Obama campaign knew that it would have to build a network of Iowans rather than supporters brought in from other parts of the country, said Plouffe, but "we didn't have to accept the electorate as it is." At bottom, Obama built a new party in 2008. It was difficult. Not until the morning of the caucuses did the campaign reach its goal of 97,000 Iowans pledged to support Obama that it thought it would need to win. Then came the real question: Would these people show up?

Show up they did, shattering turnout records. Obama prevailed with a surprising eight-point margin over Edwards, who came in second. (Clinton finished third.) Obama counted the primary in Iowa as his biggest victory, the one that foreshadowed the rest. "Voters under 30 participated at the same rates as voters over 65. That had never happened before," Obama said. "That continues to be something I'm very proud of—how [we] expanded the voter rolls in every state where [we] campaigned."

The Iowa playbook, as everyone later learned, didn't always work. In the Texas primary and caucuses this past spring, for instance, the grass-roots operation counted on more African-American voters than actually turned out. In the California primary on Super Tuesday, Feb. 5, organizers expected more young voters. But while Obama rarely managed a clean win against Clinton in the big states, he kept winning delegates even when he lost primaries. By April, it had already become almost mathematically impossible for Clinton to catch him.

THE KEY-CHAIN CAMPAIGN

Atlanta businessman Kirk Dornbush has raised millions of dollars for the Democratic Party and its candidates over the past 16 years. Before campaign-finance laws banned unregulated soft money, he recalled, there were times he walked around with six-figure checks in both pockets of his jacket. But these days, he does his fund-raising in a much humbler fashion: selling $3 key chains and $25 T shirts at Obama rallies. At the first merchandise table Dornbush set up for a Georgia event, "we were just completely sold out," he said. "There were lines of people. It was unbelievable."

Dornbush's experience explains the second fundamental change Obama brought to politics: his campaign was built from the bottom up. Even fund-raising, once the realm of the richest in politics, became a grass-roots organizational tool. At nearly every event this year, Team Obama set up little tabletop trinket shops, known as "chum stores" because all those little Obama-branded doodads aren't only keepsakes; they are also bait. Every person who bought a button or hat was recorded as a campaign donor. But the real goal of the chum operations was building a list of workers, supporters and their e-mail addresses.

A similar innovation came in fund-raising. Normally, it is only the big donors who get quality time with a candidate. But Obama devoted far more of his schedule to small-dollar events. In Kentucky, the month after he announced his run for President, the first such effort quickly sold out all 3,200 tickets at $25 a head—and produced the beginning of a local organization. "It's the difference between hunting and farming," said Obama money-man Matthew Barzun, 37, the Louisville Internet-publishing entrepreneur who arranged the event. "You plant a seed, and you get much more."

Obama uses a different frame of reference. "As somebody who had been a community organizer," Obama recalled, "I was convinced that if you invited people to get engaged, if you weren't trying to campaign like you were selling soap but instead said, 'This is your campaign, you own it, and you can run with it,' that people would respond and we could build a new electoral map." The chum stores, the e-mail obsession and the way Obama organizations sprang up organically in almost every congressional district in the country meant that by the time Obama's field organizers arrived in a state, all they had to do was fire up an engine that had already been designed and built locally. "We had to rely on the grass roots, and we had clarity on that from the beginning," said Plouffe.

By contrast, the Clinton campaign, which started out with superior resources and the mantle of inevitability, was a top-down operation in which decision-making rested with a small coterie of longtime aides. Her state organizers often got mixed signals from the headquarters near Washington. Decisions from Hillaryland often came too late for her field organization to execute. Obama's bottom-up philosophy also helped explain why he was able to sweep the organization-heavy caucus states, which were so crucial to building up his insurmountable lead in pledged delegates. What was not appreciated by many at the time: while Clinton spent heavily in every state she contested, Obama's approach saved money. Said Dean-campaign veteran Trippi: "His volunteers were organizing his caucus victories for free."

OBAMA MEANS NO DRAMA

The team that Obama put together was a mix of people who, for the most part, had never worked together before but behaved as if they had. Some—like chief strategist David Axelrod and adviser Valerie Jarrett—came from Chicago and had advised Obama in earlier races. Axelrod's business partner Plouffe had worked in former House Democratic leader Dick Gephardt's operation; deputy campaign manager Steve Hildebrand, who oversaw the field organization, had come from former Senate majority leader Tom Daschle's team. Daschle's former chief of staff Pete Rouse served that same role in Obama's Senate office, from which the candidate also brought aboard communications director Robert Gibbs, who had briefly worked for John Kerry. Obama tapped the business world as well, filling key operational posts with executives who had worked for Orbitz, McDonald's and other firms.

And yet, Obama said, they all had the same philosophy. "Because I was not favored, that meant that the people who signed up for this campaign really believed in what the campaign was about. So they weren't mercenaries. They weren't coming in to just attach to a campaign," he explained. Temperament mattered too. "It was very important to have a consistent team," Obama said, "a circle of people who were collaborative and nondefensive."

Like the team around Bush, Obama's was watertight. Leaks were rare, and for all the millions Obama raked in, Plouffe kept a sharp eye on where it was going. Consider the salaries: Clinton spokesman Howard Wolfson was paid almost twice as much in a month—$266,000 went to his firm, according to her January campaign filing—as the $144,000 that Obama paid Gibbs for all of last year. Obama staffers were expected to double up in hotel rooms when

THERE CAN ONLY BE ONE *Clinton and Obama confer in Washington shortly before she concedes the nomination*

they were on the road and were reimbursed by the campaign when they took the subway (about $2) to the downtown-Chicago campaign headquarters from O'Hare International Airport but not if they took a cab (about $50). Volunteers were asked to take along their own food when they were canvassing.

There were doubts that a team that had been living off the land could succeed against the kind of GOP operation that had been so effective at turning out the traditional Republican base four years earlier. John McCain's campaign manager, Rick Davis, flatly predicted that what got Obama the nomination would not work as "a general-election strategy" and contended that Obama's operation would be weak against McCain's crossover appeal in many key states. But compared with McCain's, Obama's operation was a model of efficiency—and executive function. Obama changed the way politics is practiced in America. After delivering his dramatic victory speech in St. Paul, Minn., after he won enough delegates to clinch his party's nomination, Obama walked offstage and spent the next 45 minutes signing dozens and dozens of his books that had been brought to the Xcel Center by admirers. When he finished, he happened to see fund raiser Dornbush and told him, "Enjoy the celebration tonight." Then Obama took a few steps, turned around and added, "But it's right back to work tomorrow."

—Originally appeared in TIME, June 16, 2008

The Overseas Test

*Obama's world tour was designed to prove that he could be
Commander in Chief. The highlight: his speech in Berlin that
was criticized at home but heard by an adoring crowd of 200,000*

By Karen Tumulty

AYING HE HAD COME TO BERLIN "NOT AS A CANDIDATE FOR PRESIDENT BUT AS A citizen—a proud citizen of the United States and a fellow citizen of the world," Barack Obama gave a soaring address on July 24, 2008, that invoked echoes of the famous speeches in this city in which John F. Kennedy made common cause with Berliners against communist oppression in 1963 and Ronald Reagan called nearly 20 years ago to tear down the Berlin Wall. "The greatest danger of all is to allow new walls to divide us from one another," Obama said to cheers from a crowd that Berlin police estimated at more than 200,000, which had gathered in the city's central park and stretched toward the Brandenburg Gate, about a mile away, where Reagan had spoken.

Obama's speech at the Victory Column was a not-so-veiled rebuke to the go-it-alone foreign policy of President Bush. He lamented that Americans and Europeans "have drifted apart and forgotten our shared destiny" rather than regarding each other as "allies who will listen to each other, learn from each other and, most of all, trust each other." He added, "I know my country has not perfected itself. We've made our share of mistakes, and there are times when our actions around the world have not lived up to our best intentions."

If it was difficult to see much difference between Obama's first trip abroad after capturing the Democratic nomination and a genuine state visit by a sitting President, well, that was sort of the point. Obama stopped in Afghanistan, Iraq, Jordan, Israel and the West Bank before heading to Germany, France and England. There was the extraordinary security at every stop:

HELLO, BERLIN *Like Kennedy and Reagan before him, Obama electrified a huge German audience*

police in Baghdad set up new roadblocks and checkpoints to secure the Iraqi capital while he was in town. There was the elaborate stagecraft: speaking at a police station in Sderot, Israel, Obama was flanked by hundreds of mortar shells, stacked in silent witness to the attacks from nearby Gaza. And there were the close, personal moments that might make a difference some-day: after Obama joined King Abdullah II for dinner at the palace in Amman, the Jordanian leader hopped into his Mercedes and drove Obama to the airport himself. Obama even flew on a refurbished Boeing 757 for the trip.

For U.S. voters, the trip was a chance to gauge how the Illinois Senator with relatively little Washington experience would perform on the world stage. In part because of the risk that voters might see the trip not as an audition but as a bold act of presumption, Obama spent much of the Iraq and Afghanistan portions of the tour joined at the hip by two fellow Senators, each with solid military credentials.

But it was Berlin that offered the most indelible, and controversial, moments. Berliners lined up to hear Obama's speech more than five hours before it began. The McCain campaign, frustrated at the media saturation of the Obama world tour, quickly put out a statement trash-ing the whole exercise. "While Barack Obama took a premature victory lap today in the heart of Berlin, proclaiming himself a 'citizen of the world,' John McCain continued to make his case to the American citizens who will decide this election." In the end, they went for Obama.

—Originally appeared on TIME.com, July 24, 2008

A day after their final debate, Obama and McCain attend a charity dinner in New York City, where they vie for the attention of Cardinal Edward Egan

April 19, 2008
Whistle-Stop Tour

*Supporters wave goodbye as Obama's campaign
train pulls out of Downington, Pa. Obama will later
lose the state's primary to Hillary Clinton*

AUG. 25, 2008
RAPT AUDIENCE

*Obama watches the TV with the Girardeau family
in Kansas City, Mo., as Michelle speaks during
Day One of the Democratic Convention*

April 22, 2008
Cutting It Close

Vying for those last votes on the day of the
Pennsylvania primary, Obama and Michelle
pose for a photo in a Philadelphia barbershop

MAY 31, 2008
WITHOUT A SCRIPT

Taking an unplanned walk after a town-hall meeting in Aberdeen, S.D., Obama surprises a family in their front yard

OCT. 16, 2008
THE FIRST COUPLE

*Less than three weeks before the election, Obama and
Michelle take time out to sit backstage at a benefit concert
by Bruce Springsteen and Billy Joel in New York City*

Ready to Lead

*Obama beat John McCain because he toned down the
big-crowd rhetoric and projected the steady, judicious
temperament Americans now crave in a President*

BY JOE KLEIN

ENERAL DAVID PETRAEUS DEPLOYED OVERWHELMING FORCE WHEN HE briefed Barack Obama and two other Senators in Baghdad last July. He knew Obama favored a 16-month timetable for the withdrawal of most U.S. troops from Iraq, and he wanted to make the strongest possible case against it. And so, after describing the current situation on the ground in great detail, Petraeus closed with a vigorous plea for "maximum flexibility" going forward. Obama had a choice at that moment. He could thank Petraeus for the briefing and promise to take his views "under advisement." Or he could tell Petraeus what he really thought, a potentially contentious course of action—especially with a general not used to being confronted. Obama chose to speak his mind. "You know, if I were in your shoes, I would be making the exact same argument," he began. "Your job is to succeed in Iraq on as favorable terms as we can get. But my job as a potential Commander in Chief is to view your counsel and interests through the prism of our overall national security." Obama talked about the deteriorating situation in Afghanistan, the financial costs of the Iraq occupation, the stress it was putting on the military.

THE TURNING POINT *At the astonishing onset of the financial crisis, it was Obama's gut steadiness that won the public trust*

A "spirited" conversation ensued, one person who was in the room told me. "It wasn't a perfunctory recitation of talking points." According to both Obama and Petraeus, the meeting ended agreeably. Petraeus said he understood that Obama's perspective was, necessarily, going to be more strategic. Obama said that the timetable obviously would have to be flexible. But the Senator had laid down his marker: if elected President, he would be in charge. Unlike George W. Bush, who had given Petraeus complete authority over the war—an unprecedented abdication of presidential responsibility—Obama would insist on a rigorous chain of command.

Obama prospered throughout the campaign because of the steadiness of his temperament and the judicious quality of his decision-making. They are his best-known qualities. But there are a thousand instantaneous decisions that a candidate has to make in the course of a campaign—like whether to speak his mind to a general—and it was often a difficult journey for Obama, since he's more comfortable when he's able to think things through. "He learned to trust his gut," an Obama adviser told me. "It's been the biggest change I've seen in him."

I asked Obama about gut decisions, in an interview on his plane 17 days before the election. It was late at night, and he looked tired, riddled with gray hair and not nearly as young as when I'd first met him four years earlier. He seemed relaxed, though, unfazed by the imminence of the vote. Our talk was informal but intense. He seemed to be thinking, rather than just reciting talking points, and it took him some time to think through my question about gut decisions. He said the first really big one was how to react when incendiary videos of the Rev. Jeremiah Wright's black-nationalist sermons surfaced. "My gut was telling me that this was a teachable moment," Obama said of the landmark speech on race relations he delivered in Philadelphia, "and that if I tried to do the usual political damage control instead of talking to the American people like . . . they were adults and could understand the complexities of race, I would be not only doing damage to the campaign but missing an important opportunity for leadership."

While Obama has followed a fairly traditional political path in this campaign, his strongest moments have occurred when he followed his natural no-drama instincts. This has been confusing to many of my colleagues and to me, at times, as well: his utter caution in the debates, his decision not to zing John McCain or even challenge him much, led me to assume that he hadn't done nearly as well as the public ultimately decided he had. But one of the more remarkable spectacles of the 2008 election was the unanimity among Democrats on matters of policy once the personality clash between Obama and Hillary Clinton was set aside. There was no squabbling between old and new Dems, progressives and moderates, over race or war or peace.

And at the crucial moment of the campaign—the astonishing onset of the financial crisis—it was Obama's gut steadiness that won the public's trust, and eventually the election. On the afternoon when McCain suspended his campaign, threatened to scuttle the Sept. 26 debate and hopped a plane to Washington to try to resolve the crisis, Obama was in Florida doing debate prep. When he was told about McCain's maneuvers, his first reaction—according to an aide—was, "You gotta be kidding. I'm going to debate. A President has to be able to do more than one thing at a time." But there was a storm brewing among Obama's supporters in the Beltway establishment. "My BlackBerry was exploding," said an aide. "They were saying we had to suspend. McCain was going to look more like a statesman, above the fray."

Obama realized that he and McCain could be little more than creative bystanders to the response to the financial crisis. He didn't have the power to influence the final outcome, so it was best to stay calm and not oversell his role. It was an easy call, his natural bias. But, Obama acknowledged, "There are going to be some times where . . . I won't have the luxury of thinking through all the angles." Which is why the Petraeus moment was so interesting. Obama's gut reaction was to go against his normal palliative impulse and to challenge the general instead. "I felt it was necessary to make that point . . . precisely because I respect Petraeus and [Ambassador Ryan] Crocker," Obama said. "Precisely because they've been doing a good job . . . And I want them to understand that I'm taking their arguments seriously."

A LMOST EXACTLY TWO YEARS AGO, I HAD MY FIRST FORMAL INTERVIEW WITH Barack Obama. It wasn't an easy one. His book *The Audacity of Hope* had just been published, but his policy proposals didn't seem very bold. But Obama seems a more certain policymaker now, if not exactly a wonk in the Clintonian sense. He has a clearer handle on the big picture, on how various policy components fit together. He wants to launch an "Apollo project" to build a new alternative-energy economy. His rationale for doing so includes some hard truths about the current economic mess. "The engine of economic growth for the past 20 years is not going to be there for the next 20," Obama said. "That was consumer spending. Basically, we turbocharged this economy based on cheap credit." A new turbocharger has to be found, and "there is no better potential driver . . . than a new energy economy . . . That's going to be my No. 1 priority."

That sort of clarity is new. The inability to describe his priorities, the inability to speak directly to voters in ways they could easily comprehend, plagued Obama through much of the primary season. His tendency to use big rhetoric in front of big crowds led to McCain's one good spell, after Obama presumptuously spoke to a huge throng in Berlin. Obama seemed to learn quickly from that mistake; his language during the general-election campaign was simple, direct and pragmatic. His best moments in the debates came when he explained what he wanted to do as President. His very best moment came in the town-hall debate when he outlined how the government bailout would affect average people who were hurting: if companies couldn't get credit from the banks, they couldn't make their payrolls and would have to start laying people off. McCain, by contrast, talked about Fannie Mae and Freddie Mac and the sins of Obama, and never brought the argument home.

As President, Obama will have to return, full force, to the inspiration business. The public will have to be mobilized to face the fearsome new economic realities. He also has to deliver bad news, transform crises into "teachable moments." He has to effect a major change in our political life: to get the public to think about long-term solutions rather than short-term balms. Obama has given some strong indications that he will be able to do this, having remained levelheaded through a season of political insanity. His was a remarkable campaign, as smoothly run as any I've seen in nine presidential cycles. Even more remarkable, Obama made race—that perennial, gaping American wound—an afterthought. He did this by introducing a quality to American politics that we hadn't seen in quite some time: maturity. He is undoubtedly as ego-driven as everyone else who has sought the highest office. But he was not childishly egomaniacal, in contrast to our recent baby-boomer Presidents—or petulant, in contrast to his opponent. He did not seem needy. He seemed a grown-up, in a nation that badly needs some adult supervision.

—Originally appeared in TIME, Nov. 3, 2008

89

The People's Choice

After a captivating campaign that rewrote the rules of American politics, Obama's stirring victory could lead to real change—if the nation's citizens are willing to get involved

BY NANCY GIBBS

S OME PRINCES ARE BORN IN PALACES. SOME ARE BORN IN MANGERS. BUT A FEW are born in the imagination, out of scraps of history and hope. Barack Obama never talks about how people see him: *I'm not the one making history,* he said every chance he got. *You are.* Yet as he looked out on election night through the bullet-proof glass, in a park named for a Civil War general, he had to see the truth on people's faces. We are the ones we've been waiting for, he liked to say, but people were waiting for him, waiting for someone to finish what a King began. "If there is anyone out there who still doubts that America is a place where all things are possible," declared the President-elect, "who still wonders if the dream of our founders is alive in our time, who still questions the power of our democracy, tonight is your answer."

Barack Obama did not win because of the color of his skin. Nor did he win in spite of it. He won because at a very dangerous moment in the life of a still young country, more people than have ever spoken before came together to try to save it. And that was a victory all its own.

Remember this day, parents told their children as they took them out of school to go see an

MAN WITH A MISSION *At Grant Park, Obama, the unlikely candidate, now the next President, tells America the victory belongs to them*

African-American candidate make history. An election in one of the world's oldest democracies looked like the kind they hold in brand-new ones, when citizens finally come out and dance, a purple-thumb day, a velvet revolution. A hundred thousand people came out in red states to hear Obama; 150,000 turned out in purple ones, even after all this time, when they should have been sick to death of Hope and Change. NASA astronauts on board the International Space Station sent a video message encouraging people to vote; they did, from 200 miles up. On the eve of the election, a Florida official locked himself in his county headquarters and slept with the ballots to make sure nothing went wrong with the vote. Early-voting lines in Atlanta were 10 hours long, and still people waited, as though their vote was their most precious and personal possession at a moment when everything else seemed to be losing its value. You heard the same phrases everywhere. *First time ever. In my lifetime. Whatever it takes.*

When it was over, more than 120 million had pulled a lever or mailed a ballot, and the system could barely accommodate Extreme Democracy. Obama won more votes than anyone else in U.S. history, the biggest Democratic victory since Lyndon Johnson crushed another Arizona Senator 44 years ago. Obama won men, which no Democrat had managed since Bill Clinton. He won 54% of Catholics, 66% of Latinos, 68% of new voters—a multicultural, multigenerational movement that shatters the old political ice pack. He let loose a deep blue wave that washed well past the coasts and the college towns: you could almost walk from Maine to Minnesota without getting your feet wet in a red state. After months of mapmaking all the roads to 270, Obama tore right past with ease.

When the race was called, there was a rush of noise, of horns honking and strangers hugging in the streets. People danced in Harlem and wept at Ebenezer Baptist Church and lit candles at Dr. Martin Luther King Jr.'s grave. More than a thousand people shouted "Yes, we can!" outside the White House, where a century ago it was considered scandalous for a President to invite a black hero to lunch. President Bush called the victory "awesome" when he phoned Obama to congratulate him: "You are about to go on one of the great journeys of life."

John McCain, freedom fighter, has always seen the nobility even—maybe especially—in a losing battle, which takes the most courage to fight. When he called Obama to concede the race, the younger man honored the elder statesman. "I need your help," Obama said, and McCain offered it without reservation. "Whatever our differences, we are fellow Americans," McCain told the crowd in a gracious speech beneath the Arizona mountains.

Remember this day. We now get to imagine, at least for a while, that the election of Obama has not just turned a page in our politics but also tossed out the whole book so we can start over. Whether by design or by default, the past now loses power: for the moment, it feels as if we've left behind the baby-boomer battles of the past 40 years; the culture wars that took us prisoner and cut us off from what we have in common; the tribal warfare between rich and poor, North and South, black and white; and the illusion, if anyone still harbored it after the past eight years, that what happens in Washington does not affect what happens everywhere else.

At a moment of obvious peril, America decided to place its fate in the hands of a man who had been born to an idealistic white teenage mother and the charismatic African grad student who abandoned them—a man who grew up without money, talked his way into good schools, worked his way up through the pitiless world of Chicago politics to the U.S. Senate and now the White House in a stunningly short period. That achievement, compared with those of the

Bushes or the Kennedys or the Adamses or any of the other American princes who were born into power or bred to it, represents such a radical departure from the norm that it finally brings meaning to the promise taught from kindergarten: "Anyone can grow up to be President."

A nation doesn't much need a big President in small times; it needs one when the future is spitting out monsters. We've heard so much about Obama's brand-new voters that we easily forget the others he found, the ones who hadn't voted since Vietnam or who had never dreamed they'd vote for a black man or a liberal or a Democrat, much less all three. But many Americans are living through the worst decade of their lives, and they have anger-management issues. They saw a war mismanaged, a city swallowed, now an economy held together with foreign loans and thumbtacks. It took a perfect storm of bad news to create this moment, but even the big men rarely win in a walk. Ronald Reagan didn't. John Kennedy didn't. Those with the clearest vision often have to fight the hardest for others to see things as they do.

O BAMA BELONGED TO A PARTY THAT WAS BENT ON RETRIBUTION; HE PREACHED reconciliation, and when voters were asked a year ago who had the best chance of winning, Hillary Clinton crushed him, 71% to 26%. He had to build a new church and reach out to those who had lost faith in government or never had any in the first place. He ran not so much on any creed as on the belief that everything was broken, that the very system that produces candidates and frames issues and decides who loses and who wins in public life does little more than make a loser out of the American people. We need to start over, he argued, listen carefully, find solutions. It was because he was an outsider with a thin résumé and few cronies or grudges that he could sell himself as the solution.

Given a President who was radioactive and an economy weak in the knees, you could say the outcome should never have been in doubt. Seventy percent more people voted in the Democratic primaries as in the Republican; 9 out of 10 people say the country is on the wrong track. In that light, McCain was his party's sacrificial lamb, a certified American hero granted one more chance to serve, with enough rebel credits on his résumé to stand a chance of winning over disgruntled voters if Obama somehow imploded. While it may not have been much of a race in the end, it certainly was a choice: not just black and white or red and blue or young and old. Over time, it has become clear that these men view change very differently. McCain sees change as an ordeal, a test of his toughness; Obama sees it as an opportunity, a test of his versatility.

Yet Obama, derided as so ethereal compared with the battle-tested McCain, was the clear-eyed realist in the room; he was a child of change—changed countries, cultures, careers, even his name: Barry became Barack. You can't stop change from coming, he argued; you can only usher it in and work out the terms. If you're smart and a little lucky, you can make it your friend.

As if that choice hadn't been clear enough, McCain drew the lines a little brighter. The Veep selection always promised to be complicated for a solo pilot who resisted the idea of a partner at every turn, but now the Constitution required him to pick a wingman. And if anyone imagined that we'd make it through an entire general election without an all-out culture war, Sarah Palin's arrival took care of it. She called herself a fresh face who couldn't wait to take on the good ole boys. But far from framing the future, Palin played deep chords from the past—the mother of five from a frontier town who invoked the values of a simpler, safer America than the globally competitive, fiscally challenged, multicultural marketplace of ideas where Obama lived. She seemed to delight in the contrast and talked of the "real America," the "pro-America areas of this great nation." It was an invitation for Obama to show how far the country had come. "There are no real or fake parts of this country," he fired back. "We are one nation, all of us proud, all of us patriots . . ."

STILL, AS OF MID-SEPTEMBER, MCCAIN, WITH PALIN AT HIS SIDE, HAD CLOSED THE gender gap, ignited his base and seemed to be having fun for the first time in ages. He hammered the point that he was the only one who had been tested in a crisis. It was working great—until he was tested in a crisis. The assumption all year was that if the Furies delivered turmoil to the doorstep of this election, the country would retreat to the safe choice and not risk a rookie. It was Obama's triumph that the financial crisis that might have buried him actually raised him up, let voters judge his judgment in real time. It gave him, over the course of three weeks and three debates, a stage for statesmanship that decades of Senate debate could never have offered.

On the day Lehman Brothers evaporated, McCain was running 2 points ahead. In September, when the *Wall Street Journal* asked people who was better on taxes, McCain beat Obama, 41% to 37%. Over the next month, there was an 18-point swing, until Obama prevailed on taxes, 48% to 34%. The Obama campaign never missed a chance to replay McCain's quotes about the fundamentals of the economy being strong or that he was "fundamentally a deregulator" at a time when regulation was fundamentally overdue. The moment McCain tried to seize the moment, suspend the campaign and ride back to Washington to rescue the global financial system only to be shut down by his own party, he handed Obama a weapon almost as powerful as the crisis itself. Times were suddenly scary—and McCain was "erratic," "impulsive," reckless. He fell into a trap he couldn't get out of for weeks. Every time McCain took a swing, as his cheering section demanded he do, those undecided-voter dial meters plunged. Six in 10 voters said McCain was spending more time attacking Obama than explaining his own positions.

Over the course of three debates right in the heat of the crisis, voters got to take the measure of the men directly—no stadium crowds, no stunts, no speechwriters to save them. They were being told that Obama was a dangerous radical who hung out with terrorists. Simply by seeming sober and sensible, he both reassured voters and diminished McCain, whose attacks seemed disingenuous. A New York *Times* survey found that people who changed their views on Obama were twice as likely to say they had grown more favorable, not less; those who now saw McCain differently were three times as likely to say their view had worsened than had improved. By mid-October, only 1 in 3 voters thought McCain would bring the country a real change in direction. He never got close again.

By the end, some lessons were already clear. Obama's brute financial force, outspending McCain nearly 2 to 1, guarantees that the way we pay for our politics will never be the same— and money and power tend to flow as one. A new generation of voters are about to show us whether they dropped in to visit or intend to stay. The Democrats in Congress were handed greater power despite abiding unpopularity; we'll now see whether they understand that it's a loan, not a reward. And the repudiation of President Bush and his allies ensures that the conservative movement will have to sit in a circle, hold hands, light some incense and figure out what its members really believe in when it comes to putting their principles into practice.

MEET THE OBAMAS *The next First Family takes the stage to acknowledge the election-night crowd*

As for Obama, which Democrats will he side with? The old Ted Kennedy liberals he re-inspired, the Blue Dogs he courted, the new arrivals from purple and even red districts whose shelf life depends on a centrist agenda? He has talked about the need to fix entitlements, but try to pin him down on the Audacity of How, and he vanishes in a foam of contingency. He voted for the $700 billion Wall Street bailout, but there are bound to be far more claims on that pot than there is money available in it. Obama has had teams of people already working with the Treasury Department and the Pentagon in the event of a victory. At a time like this, there's probably no such thing as being overprepared.

His vow to bring people together will mean nothing if he just does what's easy. He has to find real Republicans to put in real Cabinet positions, not just Transportation. He needs to use his power in ways that make the two parties equally unhappy, to dust off the weighty words we need to hear—like austerity, sacrifice, duty to the children we keep borrowing from. "This victory alone is not the change we seek," he told the nation on election night. "It is only the chance for us to make that change. And that cannot happen if we go back to the way things were."

We get the leaders we deserve. And if we lift them up and then cut them off, refuse to follow unless they are taking us to Disneyland, then no President, however historic his mandate or piercing his sense of what needs to be done, can take us where we refuse to go. This did not all end on Election Day, Obama said again and again as he talked about the possibility of ordinary people doing extraordinary things. And so, we are merely at the end of the beginning.

—WITH REPORTING BY LAURA FITZPATRICK

—Originally appeared in TIME, Nov. 17, 2008